EVERYDAY RELIGION

My Jewish Life

Anne Clark and David Rose

WAYLAND

EVERYDAY RELIGION

My Buddhist Life
My Christian Life
My Hindu Life
My Jewish Life
My Muslim Life
My Sikh Life

Editor: Ruth Raudsepp
Designer: Joyce Chester

First published in 1996 by Wayland Publishers Ltd, 61 Western Road,
Hove, East Sussex, BN3 1JD, England.

British Library Cataloguing in Publication Data
Clark, Anne
My Jewish Life – (Everyday Religion)
1. Judaism – Juvenile literature 2. Jews – Juvenile literature
I. Title II. Rose, David W.
296
ISBN 0-7502-1299-3

Picture acknowledgements
All the photographs were taken by David Rose with the exception of Zefa *cover;* 12 and 22.
The authors would like to thank the following who were photographed for this book:
Emily Altneu; Melanie, Barry and Jordan Angel; the Bower Ish-Horowicz family,
particularly Joanna and Michal; Malcolm and Michael Clark; Rabbi Nissan Dubov and
Leah Dubov; Tonia Hayes; Lia, Tim, Sarah and Ben Kahn-Zajtmann; David Malyan;
Helena and Arieh Miller; Rabbi Sylvia Rothschild and Charlotte Rothschild; Rabbi Robert
Shafritz; Alma and Micah Smith; Sophie and Andrew Sweetman; Olivia Sweiry; Elise,
Martin, Sarah and Paul Wolfson; Lily, David, Michael and Jonathan Zoubaida; members
of North West Surrey and Wimbledon and District Synagogues.
Thanks also to Bebe Jacobs and Clive Lawton for their helpful comments on the manuscript.

Typeset by Joyce Chester
Printed in Italy by G. Canale S.p.A.

Contents

The Mezuzah 5

Jewish Symbols 6

Simchat Torah 7

The Torah 8–9

Bar Mitzvah 10–11

A Jewish Wedding 12

Blessing a Baby 13

Shabbat 14–15

Pesach 16–17

Hanukkah 18–19

The Western Wall, Jerusalem 20–21

Purim 22–23

Shopping for Jewish Food 24

Rosh Hashanah 25

Sukkot 26

Remembrance 27

Notes for Teachers 28–29

Glossary 30–31

Books to Read 31

Index 32

These children are all
Jews. There are Jews
all over the world.
It is like being part of
one big family.

Leah's father is lifting her up so that she can touch the **mezuzah**, which contains words from the **Torah**.

Emily and David are helping to make a special picture for Jewish New Year.

On **Simchat Torah** Jewish children say a blessing over the Torah. They gather around the Torah underneath a prayer shawl called a **tallit**.

The Torah scrolls are kept in a special cupboard called the Ark. The light above it stays on all the time.

This lady is a **rabbi**. She and her daughter, Charlotte, are reading the Torah using a special pointer called a yad.

Michael and Malcolm are getting the Torah scroll ready to read at their **Bar Mitzvah**.

Michael is watching as his brother Malcolm reads in **Hebrew** from the Torah scroll.

Jewish people get married under
a special canopy, or cover, called
a huppah.

This mother and father have come to the **synagogue** to thank God for their baby. The rabbi is blessing baby Jordan.

Shabbat is a special day for Jewish people. It starts at sunset on Friday evening. After lighting candles the family eat a meal together.

At the end of Shabbat, Jewish people light a **havdalah** candle and say goodbye to Shabbat for another week.

Do you know why Jonathan and his family eat special food at **Pesach**? It helps them tell the story of how God freed the Jews from Egypt.

Jonathan has found the **afikomen** which his father hid at the beginning of the **seder**.

Tonight is the last night of **Hanukkah**. Ben and his family are lighting all eight candles on their **hanukiah** using a servant candle.

Ben and his sister Sarah are playing
a Hanukkah game with a spinning
top called a **dreidel**.

These Jews are praying at the Western Wall in Jerusalem. Jews have prayed to God here for thousands of years.

Some Jewish boys come from all over the world to have their Bar Mitzvah at the Western Wall. Their families and friends are watching.

Purim is a happy festival. Many
Jewish children wear fancy dress.

Purim is also a time for sharing.
Sophie and Andrew give some fruit
and special Purim cakes to their
friend, Tonia.

Arieh is helping his mother buy the special foods which Jewish people eat.

On **Rosh Hashanah** Alma and
Micah eat slices of apple dipped in
honey. They are hoping for a sweet
New Year.

During the festival of **Sukkot**
Jewish people eat all their meals in
a **sukkah**.

Joanna and Michal are thinking about their Great Grandmother who died a year ago. Jews light a candle each year to remember people in their family who have died.

Notes for Teachers

p5 The mezuzah is a small container attached to the right-hand doorposts of Jewish homes, synagogues and shops. It contains part of the Shema which is written on parchment by a scribe. The first line of the Shema (Hear O Israel... Deuteronomy 6 v 4) may be described as a central declaration of faith. It affirms the monotheistic nature of Judaism. Some Jewish people touch the mezuzah with a kiss whenever passing.

p6 Many children who do not go to Jewish schools attend supplementary classes on a Sunday morning and/or after school during the week. Here they receive Jewish religious education which may include Hebrew language classes, study of the Torah and Jewish history, and the celebration of Jewish culture and festivals. In this picture, the children are making a frieze for the children's service at Rosh Hashanah. The symbols seen here are a fish, a Torah scroll and scales which symbolize the idea of God weighing up our actions.

p7 On Simchat Torah the annual cycle of Torah readings is completed and restarted. The last section of Deuteronomy is read, and then the first portion of Genesis is immediately read. This symbolizes continuity and unity. The ceremony is rich with the symbolism of marriage. Two members of the synagogue, called the bridegroom of the Torah and the bridegroom of Genesis, are given the honour of reading the last and first sections of the Torah. In this photo the children have been invited to share in the blessings being said over the Torah. They are standing beneath a tallit, just as a bride and groom will stand beneath the huppah (pronounced hoo-pa).

p8 The Ark, or receptacle where the Torah is kept, is usually set in the wall facing Jerusalem. The Ark is the focal point of every synagogue and it is a reminder of the wilderness wanderings when the Ten Commandments were kept in a portable ark inside the Tabernacle. Above every Ark may be seen the Ner Tamid, the everburning light symbolizing the presence of God. In many synagogues the Ark is beautifully set behind embroidered curtains with Hebrew writing above. This key sentence seen here tells the worshipper, 'Know before Whom you stand'.

p9 The Torah scroll is written by hand on parchment made from a kosher animal, i.e. permitted by Jewish dietary laws. It contains the Pentateuch, the Five Books of Moses. It is written in Hebrew and laid out in columns and is read from right to left. The text is never touched by the human hand. A yad is used instead to point to the words being read.

p10 Before the scroll is read, it needs to be 'undressed'. Here the rimmonim are being removed. They are placed on a special holder which can be seen. The rimmonim and other 'ornaments' on the Torah scroll are reminiscent of items worn by the High Priest during the period of the Tabernacle and Temple.

p11 During his Bar Mitzvah Malcolm stands on a raised dais called the bimah and uses the yad to read from the Torah. He is wearing a kippah (skull cap) and tallit, as is his twin brother. Beside him can be seen the traditional blessings which are chanted before and after each section of the Torah reading. Here Malcolm reads from the beginning of the scroll.

p12 At a Jewish wedding the ceremony takes place under a huppah. This canopy is often decorated with flowers. It is a symbol of the Jewish home which the couple will 'build' together. Marriage and family life are seen as having supreme importance within Jewish tradition for the transmission of Jewish belief and values.

p13 There are variations in customs surrounding the birth of a baby between Orthodox and Progressive Jewish communities. In both communities all boys receive their Jewish names when they are circumcised at eight days of age. In Progressive synagogues baby naming ceremonies generally take place during the Shabbat morning service. In Orthodox communities there is a thanksgiving prayer during the service for girls on the Shabbat following their birth. Often the names chosen for boys and girls are Biblical characters or those of deceased members of the family. In this photo the order of service being followed is from the siddur (prayer book).

p14 Shabbat is welcomed each week in the family by the lighting of two candles and the reciting of a prayer called kiddush. Blessings are said over the wine and the bread which are then shared. The two loaves called challot (pronounced hallot) are eaten after being sprinkled with salt. See Exodus chapter 16 v 22ff, which refers to the double portion of manna signified by the challot.

p15 Shabbat ends with the family joining in the ceremony of havdalah. The lighting of a plaited candle marks the transition between the 'rest' of Shabbat and the work of the weekdays. A spice box, here in the shape of a tower, is passed around. The spices symbolize the 'sweetness' of Shabbat which Jews wish to take into the working week. The wine is a symbol of God's blessing. Havdalah involves the whole family and all the senses are brought into play.

p16 The highlight of Pesach is the seder meal at which the Exodus from Egypt is symbolically re-enacted. It involves the whole family (including extended family). The Hagadah is the book used during the seder. Its contents include the order of the service and the details of the Exodus. Notice the symbolic foods on the seder plate which include parsley, a roast egg, roast bone and a sweet paste called haroset. This family uses lemon juice rather than salt water to symbolize the tears of slavery.

p17 During the seder the children search for the piece of matzah (unleavened bread), called the afikomen, hidden by the seder leader earlier on. The seder is very child-orientated and is used as a means of effectively transmitting Jewish traditions from generation to generation. Here Jonathan shows his delight at having found the afikomen, because he can expect to barter for a 'reward', as the seder cannot be completed until after the afikomen is eaten.

p18 Hanukkah is the Jewish festival of light. It celebrates the period of the Maccabees in the 2nd century BCE when the Jews were freed from religious persecution and the Temple in Jerusalem was rededicated. Jewish families celebrate Hanukkah by lighting the nine branched hanukiah, eating special foods such as potato latkes (pancakes) and doughnuts, exchanging presents and playing special games.

p19 The game of dreidel involves spinning a four-sided spinning top. On each side there is a Hebrew letter which together form the initials of the phrase 'a great miracle happened there'. The rules of the game are simple and enjoyed by children of all ages. Whilst Jewish observance and Torah study was forbidden at the time of the Maccabees, the Jews continued to do these things in secret. Legend has it that they played with the dreidel to hide these activities, especially when it was thought there were enemies or spies about.

p20 The Western Wall is the only part of the Temple in Jerusalem remaining today. It is a place of prayer and pilgrimage. Many Jews write their petitions to God on pieces of paper and place them in the cracks in the Wall. Jews from several communities can be seen here. Note in the photo the long coat and black hat – distinguishing clothing of the hasidim.

p21 As in an Orthodox synagogue, men and women pray separately at the Western Wall. This photo shows family Bar Mitzvah groups. Due to the significance of the location, many Jews will travel to Jerusalem for their Bar Mitzvah.

p22 On Purim Jews celebrate the intervention of the Jewish heroine Esther who managed to save the Jewish people from persecution. Her story is told in the Megillah, the scroll of Esther. Purim is a time for special foods, fancy dress and puppets and letting one's hair down!

p23 According to the book of Esther (chapter 9 v 22) the Purim celebration should include giving charity to the poor and exchanging gifts of food (mishloach manot) with friends. Each festival and life cycle event in Judaism provides an opportunity to give to others.

p24 Jewish dietary laws occupy a central place in Jewish tradition. There are strict regulations with regard to what foods may be eaten and how they are prepared. The term 'kosher' is applied to these types of foods. In areas with a large Jewish population there are kosher food shops.

p25 Rosh Hashanah, Jewish New Year, is a time for reflection and resolution. All the members of the family celebrate with the eating of apple dipped in honey to symbolize their hopes for a 'sweet' new year. On the table can be seen a greetings card, a shofar (ram's horn) and the two round challot used at festivals instead of the usual plaited loaves.

p26 The most important part of a sukkah is the roof which is made of cut branches and must be open to the sky. Jewish children enjoy decorating the sukkah with fruit and with their own artwork.

p27 The family is an important unit and there are several opportunities during the year to remember the dead, both at home and in the synagogue. The yahrzeit, or memorial candle, is lit each year on the anniversary of the death of close relatives. This burns for at least 24 hours. For Jewish families this effectively keeps memories alive.

Glossary

afikomen Dessert. A piece of matzah eaten near the end of the seder.

Bar Mitzvah A boy's coming of age at 13 years old. Bar Mitzvah means Son of Commandment. Bat Mitzvah is a girl's coming of age from 12 years old. Bat Mitzvah means Daughter of Commandment.

dreidel A spinning top with four sides, with a Hebrew letter on each side.

hanukiah A lamp with nine branches used at the festival of Hanukkah.

Hanukkah An eight-day festival of lights celebrating the rededication of the temple by the Maccabees.

havdalah The ceremony marking the end of Shabbat.

Hebrew The language of the Torah and Jewish prayer books. Also the everyday language in Israel.

mezuzah A scroll placed on doorposts of Jewish buildings, containing a section from the Torah and often enclosed in a decorative case.

Pesach The festival when Jews remember the Exodus from Egypt.

Purim The festival celebrating the rescue of the Jews, as told in the book of Esther.

rabbi A Jewish religious teacher and leader.

Rosh Hashanah Jewish New Year.

seder A ceremonial meal in Jewish homes on Pesach during which the story of the Exodus from Egypt is told.

Shabbat Jewish day of rest which begins at sunset on Friday and ends at nightfall on Saturday.

Simchat Torah The festival which celebrates completing the reading of the Torah and starting again.

sukkah A temporary shelter in which Jews eat and sometimes sleep during Sukkot.

Sukkot An eight-day festival commemorating the time when the Jews journeyed in the wilderness.

synagogue The building used by Jews for meeting, study and prayer.

tallit A prayer shawl.

Torah The first five books of the Bible.

Books to Read

Greer Cashman, *Jewish Days and Holidays*, Adama Books, 1986.

Judith Gross, *Celebrate – A Book of Jewish Holidays*, Platt & Munk, 1992.

Sandy Lanton, *Daddy's Chair*, Kar-Ben Copies, 1990.
During the Jewish week of mourning a young boy begins to come to terms with his father's death.

Eric Ray, *Sofer: The Story of a Torah Scroll*, Torah Aura Productions, 1986. A Jewish scribe explains how he writes and prepares Torah scrolls, tefillin and mezuzot.
Black and white photographs, plus large Hebrew letters for children to trace or copy.

Note on Dates

Each religion has its own system for counting the years of its history. The starting point may be related to the birth or death of a special person or an important event. In every day life, today, when different communities have dealings with each other, they need to use the same counting system for setting dates in the future and writing accounts of the past. The Western system is now used throughout the world. It is based on Christian beliefs about Jesus: AD (Anno Domini = in the year of our Lord) and BC (Before Christ). Members of the various world faiths use the common Western system, but, instead of AD and BC, they say and write CE (in the Common Era) and BCE (before the Common Era).

Due to certain requirements of Jewish law, some situations shown here were specially created for this book.

The words in transliteration have been spelt in accordance with the recommendations of the SCAA Glossary of Terms for Religious Education.

Index

afikomen 17, 30
Ark, the 8

Bar Mitzvah 10, 21, 30

dreidel 19, 30

hanukiah 18, 30
Hanukkah 18, 19, 30
havdalah 15, 30
Hebrew 11, 30

Jerusalem 20

marriage 12
mezuzah 5, 30

New Year, Jewish 6, 25, 30

Pesach 16, 30
Purim 22, 23, 30

rabbi 9, 30
Rosh Hashanah 25, 30

seder 17, 30
Shabbat 14, 15, 31

Simchat Torah 7, 31
sukkah 26, 31
Sukkot 26, 31
synagogue 13, 31

tallit 7, 31
Torah 5, 7, 8, 9, 10, 11, 31

Western Wall 20, 21

yad 9